Get "Twitter"pated
A Writer's Handbook to Twitter

Jen Nipps

GenXt Press
Ada, Oklahoma

Get Twitter-pated: A Writer's Handbook to Twitter (2nd edition)

© Jen Nipps

No part of this book may be reproduced without the written permission of the author.

KDP/GenXt Press
Jen Nipps
Ada, Oklahoma
www.jennippsonline.com

Orders: jennippsonline@gmail.com

ISBN-13: 9781726890052

Jen Nipps

For Mom.
You helped me find the final piece of the puzzle to pull this together.

Table of Contents

Introduction	5
Why Twitter?	7
Hash It out: The Power of Hashtags	16
Twitter Do's & Don'ts from People Who Have Been There	25
Twitter Applications	29
Benefitting from & Adding Value to Twitter	33
Avoiding the Time-Sink	40
Your First Tweets	44
Appendix A	47
Appendix B	49
Appendix C	50
Appendix D	52
About the Author	59
Other Books By Jen Nipps	60
Connect with Jen Online	61

Jen Nipps

Introduction

No matter what we do in life, there are typically three ways to approach something new:

1. With hesitance. After all, something new means change and change is never good. Right?
2. With enthusiasm. Jumping in with both feet is all well and good, but sometimes it's helpful to know how deep or cold the water is first.
3. With careful planning and determination. The temperature of the water has been determined. It's ten feet deep. The currently is slow. It's swimmable.

Regardless of which approach you take, you've picked a good place to start. Information. Experience from someone who has "been there, done that." Advice from a few Twitter/social media experts.

In short, this book.

If you're scared to start something new, think of this as me holding your hand, guiding you through the steps of getting Twitterpated.

If you tend to jump in with both feet, let me hold you back a little bit and get you to think about some things you might have overlooked in your haste to sign up for the next big thing.

If you prefer to do research and plan your course of action, good for you. You'll find steps, tips, and advice from Twitter users, social media experts, and myself.

This is set up as a workbook. If you have a print copy, feel free to write on the lines and mark it up in whichever way best suits you. If you have a Kindle copy, have a pen and paper ready so you can answer the questions and do the exercises for yourself as you come to them.

By the way, if you have Twitter-related questions as we're going along in this book, feel free to email me at jennippsonline@gmail.com or follow me on Twitter at http://www.twitter.com/JenNipps and ask me there.

Now let's get started.

Chapter 1
Why Twitter?

First things first: Why do you want to be on Twitter? If you said because your friends are or to socialize or because it's the next big thing, you need to reevaluate your Twitter presence.

All social media is about making connections. That's where the social part comes in.

Imagine Twitter as being like the professional networking events you can go to through your local Chamber of Commerce or the meet-and-greets you participate in at writers' conferences.

You have a product to sell (your manuscript), but that isn't your primary purpose for being there. If you happen to make a sale in the process, so much the better, but your reason for going to the event is to make contacts.

That is where Twitter is most valuable. It's also where Twitter is most overwhelming.

Out of all the people on Twitter, how do you know who to connect with? Let's face it: If you try to connect with everyone on Twitter, you're opening yourself up to spam, people and companies irrelevant to who you are and what you do, and a lot of "noise" in your Twitter feed.

> *What's This?*
>
> A **Twitter feed,** or stream, is the page of Tweets from everyone you follow on Twitter. You see it when you click on the home page after you log in.

Determining Your Purpose

When I talk to people about Twitter, online and off, I ask why they want to be on this particular social media platform. Sometimes they will say they want to keep in touch with friends and family. To them, I recommend Facebook. However, more often than not, they say, "To make contacts."

All right. That's a good reason. But it's too broad. They—and you—need to narrow it down. Why do you want to make contacts?

Do you have a book to sell? Are you a freelance writer and/or journalist looking for sources. Are you in public relations and need to set up an account for your employer or your clients?
Use this space to write out your purpose for being on Twitter.

_____
_____
_____
_____
_____

Now we're getting somewhere.

What is your book about? Use Twitter Search to search for your topic (or topics) in the Twitter Stream. Participate in some discussions and find some people you think are interesting to follow. Contribute some information about your topic and you will gain followers that way as well. However, constantly saying you have a book available for people to buy and here's the link for it is considered Twitter spam and will not get you any connections. You need and want to be genuine, share information, and answer questions to be of and receive value from Twitter for it to be beneficial to you.

What's This?

Twitter Search is Twitter's own search engine that looks for keywords among any and all public Tweets. If someone's account is private, it will not pick up on those Tweets unless it's someone you follow. You can go directly to Twitter Search at http://search.twitter.com.

After you have been on Twitter for a while and have developed a good following, which is defined by you, then you might be able to start mentioning your book and providing a link every so often, but not more than once a day.

What if your book's subject is a general topic? What then? You have to figure out if you're willing to have a general following or if you want to narrow it down to what you think the book's primary focus is.

I know what you're thinking. This is all well and good for book authors, but what about freelance writers and journalists?

You have it easier than the book people. You generally have three or four topic areas that you cover the most. Follow the same process given above to find people in your areas of expertise. The same goes for public relations people, though you have the added task of finding and listening to customers/clients of your employer or client and monitoring public opinion.

Good. You know why you're on Twitter and you have defined your purpose. Let's keep going.

Getting Started

Before you can jump right into the Twitter stream, you need to finish the basics for swimming in it. That is, you need to fill out your profile to go with what your purpose is. This will make it easier when people find you to know that you *are* who they want to follow.

The first thing you need is your username. Now, if you jumped the gun and got on Twitter before you figured out your purpose, you already have that. It's not too late to change it if you decide to do that, though.

I recommend using a variation of your name, if it's available. Let's face it: If JenNipps is ever taken, it's because I signed up somewhere in the past and forgot about it, so mine was relatively easy. Think about several different variations in case your preferred one is taken. If your name is Jane Doe and you're a writer, you're in luck. The username "janedoewriter" is available. So is "authorjanedoe." However, if you wanted to go with just "janedoe," that username is not available on Twitter.

If you prefer not to use your given name as your username, choose one that describes what you do. For example, Linda Apple is an inspirational writer. Instead of using her given name as her Twitter username, she uses "write_2_inspire," which is a perfect description of what she does.

Generally when you choose your username, you also have to decide on a password and provide a valid email address. The email address is for verification purposes and if you choose to receive Twitter notifications. Make sure the password is one you can remember while also being a combination of numbers and letters to lessen the possibility of your account being hacked or phished.

Yes, it happens. Yes, there are things you can do to avoid it. Basically, do not ever use your children's names or your pet's name as your password anywhere online. Some people recommend changing your password every so often. I'm not a huge advocate of that, because I forget to do it myself.

For right now, let me walk you through the steps of setting you your Twitter profile. If you don't have access to a computer right now, that's all right. Write in the spaces provided and type it in Twitter later.

When you're on the screen to edit your profile, you'll see several options: Account, Password, Mobile, Notices, Profile, Design, and Connections. Starting with the Account page, make certain your username is spelled the way you mean for it to be. Typos happen and if you reverse two letters and don't catch it, you'll have difficulty logging in to your account.

Give three options for your username in case your preferred one is already taken.

_____
_____
_____

What email address will you be using for Twitter? Under the box for this, there is a check-box with a question of if you want others to be able to find you by your email address or not. At no time will your email address be publicly visible on the site unless you yourself put it in a Tweet or in your bio, which is not recommended.

_____
_____

What's This?

A **Tweet** is a post on Twitter. It's limited to 280 characters, including spaces and punctuation. When you reply to someone, their username is above the Tweet box and those characters are not counted. (In the first edition of this book, the character limit was 140 characters and usernames did count toward the character limit. Neither of those is the case anymore.)

The remainder of the Account page asks for your preferred language, time zone, and if you want to add a location to your tweets. Personally, I recommend against adding a location, but it's dependent on your purpose for Twitter and your own personal comfort level. If you have a physical business for customers to come in, by all means, add a location. On the bottom of this page, you can select whether or not to see media (videos, music, pictures, etc.) from everyone on Twitter or just the people you follow.

You can also choose to make your profile private. I've gone back and forth on the issue of private profiles. When your profile is private, you tweets are essentially locked and not viewable to anyone who you do not follow. At this point, I recommend against making your profile private. You have a product to sell; you don't want to lock out the majority of your potential customer base or audience.

We're finished with the Account page. To to Password. You've already got this set up unless this is your first encounter with Twitter. You don't need this page right now unless you want to change it. Move on to Mobile.

On the Mobile page, you have the option of entering your mobile phone number so you can receive text messages of tweets. This uses what they call SMS, or short message service. If you choose to have this turned on, do not enable it for everyone or you will be flooded with text messages. Before you turn it on for anyone, check with your mobile service provider and see what your texting plan is. If you do not have unlimited texts, do not enable this option. If you do decide to go with the Mobile option, you can choose if you want to turn the service off between certain hours. There is also a check box asking if you want people to be able to find you by your phone number. I recommend that you say no to that, so uncheck the box. Be sure to click the save button if you've made any changes to this page.

NOTE: In the first edition of this book, smart phones were not as readily available as they are now. Many of the references made to the Mobile page may well be obsolete with the popularity of smart phones and various apps for Twitter.

Now we're ready for the Notices page. If you want to receive email when you get new followers or when you receive a new direct message, make sure the boxes are checked. The last check box on that page asks whether or not you want to receive emails about what's going on with Twitter. Personally, I receive more than enough email, so I unchecked the box so I do *not* get those emails.

What's This?

Direct Messages (DMs) are Twitter's private in-site message service. You can use this feature on the web-based server or on your preferred Twitter app on your smart phone.

Now we're to the fun part: The Profile page.

When you sign up on Twitter, you get a default avatar. I've seen it be the Twitter bird icon, an oval in a square, or a pair of "googly" eyes that look something like this: o_O.

Please do not keep the default avatar you are given. It is more likely that you will get positive feedback and more followers if you upload a picture of yourself or (if you have one) your logo. I have used a picture of me and my book(s), professional headshots, a candid photo of me, and my logo.

Twitter has specifications for your picture, so be careful that you don't choose one so large that, when it's cropped, you lose your head or one so small that when it's enlarged, you see every pixel that makes up the photo.

Do you want a different name to show on just your profile, not on your tweets, than your username? The box under the picture is where you can put it. What is it?

_____

_____

The next box is for your location. This one can be general. I just put "Oklahoma" or "south-central Oklahoma" since that's where I live. You don't have to put anything here. It can be left blank.

Do you have a website? If you don't, I highly recommend that you get one. Or, at the very least, get a blog and put the address to it in this box. My blog is on my website, so if you click my website link, it will take you to the blog page. What is your website or your blog address?

Twitter has saved the best for last. The box for your bio is last on this page. Remember how your tweets are limited to 280 characters, including spaces and punctuation? You don't have much more room for your bio.

Think carefully and write tight. What do you want to say about yourself? Act like you're taking an essay test in high school and you had to go back and count your words. Instead, you have to count your letters, numbers, punctuation, and spaces. When you enter it on Twitter, don't forget to click "save." (I've done that before. That's why I keep reminding you.)

Ta da! At this point, you can stop because your profile is finished. However, if you want to play with the design of your profile, go to the Design page. Twitter has provided some options for you to choose from. Just because they provide the options doesn't mean you have to use any of them.

Do you have a different picture on you computer that you would rather use? Upload your picture! At one time, my background was a spiral notebook page. I didn't change it for quite some time. Select a color scheme that goes with the background you've chosen. When you make your choices call a friend or email me and ask someone to check it out and see if it's readable.

Now you *are* done. The only page left is Connections. (Now it's called Applications, I think.) If you use a Twitter application, such as Twitpic for pictures or a chat client, those will show up on this page. If you ever decide you would rather not use them, you can go to this page and remove their permissions.

See? Was that as hard as you thought it would be? You're ready to get into the nuts and bolts of Twitter. Let's talk about hashtags next, because you'll see them a lot.

Chapter 2
Hash It out: The Power of Hashtags

If you've looked around Twitter any, you've likely seen then. Hashtags. They're little links in blue (or whatever your color scheme uses) with a "#" in front of them.

What's This?

A **hashtag** enables tweets to be searched more easily with the Twitter Search. There are some Twitter clients that use hashtags, which we'll talk about in a minute.

Such tags are the basis for many communities on Twitter. There are also some webinars and conferences online that use hashtags to track the discussion and participants' feedback. Some notable ones (past and present) include:

#IFD10 (and #IFD11): Independent Freelancers Day 2010, which included presentations from Ed Gandia, Mari Smith, and others. The organizers anticipate this to be an annual event. Look for #IFD109 and so on in the following years. (It appears #IFD also is used by I'll Fight Day, so beware of other organizations/movements using similar hashtags.)

#BWE10 (and so on): Blog World & New Media Expo 2010. Mark Burnett, Doug Ulman, and Mark Penn were among the keynote speakers. This is an annual event. They have also used the hashtag #BWE09. (Again, this is a case of other organizations using similar hashtags. In this case, it's Boston Wine Expo.)

Twitter Chats

There are also long-standing Twitter communities that come together once a week or so for regularly scheduled chats. Currently, there are over 500 chats hosted on Twitter. Of these, several are (and have been) specifically for writers.

#Blogchat
Billed as "the largest chat on Twitter," Blogchat aims to help writers improve their blogging efforts, be they personal or business. On the first Sunday of the month, cohosts join the chat. The last Sunday of the month is Open Mic where the chat participants pick the topic.
Host: Mack Collier (@mackcollier)
Time: 8:00 to 9:00 CST on Sundays
Website: http://www.mackcollier.com/social-media-library/what-is-blogchat

#bookmarket
The aim of this chat is to connect authors, publishers, bloggers, and publicists "for the greater good." Topics have included self-publishing.
Host: Claudia Christianson (@ClaudiaC)
Time: 4:00 to 5:00 EST on Thursdays

#fantasychat
Fantasy writers get together every week for this chat. They discuss all topics that are involved in writing fantasy novels.

Hosts: Marilyn Muniz (@marilymuniz) and Keri Wright (@fantasychat)
Time: 8:00 to 9:00 PST on Sundays
Website: http://tagdef.com/fantasychat

#followreader
This chat is for readers, publishers, authors, librarians, book bloggers, and "anyone else interested and invested in the bookish community."
Hosts: Kat Meyer (@katmeyer) and Charlotte Abbott (@charabbott)
Time: 4:00 to 5:00 PM EST on Fridays
Website: http://followthereader.wordpress.com

#journchat
Journchat was started by Sarah Evans (@PRSarahEvans) to bring journalists, bloggers, and public relations professionals together for a weekly conversation. On the site, Evans said, "#journchat is a SAFE environment where all can freely post questions and answers. Constructive criticism and 'brutal facts' are welcome! The quali6ty of dialogue in each session is only as good as those who participate."
Hosts: Sarah Evans (@PRSarahEvans) and @journchat
Time: 8:00 to 9:00 EST on Mondays
Website: http://journchat.info
NOTE: #journchat is no longer active. I decided to keep it here because you can still search the hashtag and find useful information.

#kidlitchat
Participants talk about everything from board books to Young Adult literature in this weekly chat. A related chat for illustrators is #kidlitartchat, but is not hosted by the same people.
Hosts: Bonnie Adamson (@BonnieAdamson) and Greg Pincus (@gregpincus)
Time: 9:00 PM EST on Tuesdays

#poetrychatparty
This chat includes published poets and editors as guests to filed questions. There are also opportunities to create poems.
Host: @32poems (The editors of *32 Poems*, a print poetry magazine)
Time: 9:00 to 10:00 PM EST on Sundays

#poetry
"We talk poetry." The chat welcomes readers and writers. Others are encouraged to join as well.
Host: Greg Pincus (@gregpincus)
Time: 8:00 to 9:00 PM CST on Thursdays

#romancechat
This chat advertises that participants discuss "all things romantic in writing."
Hosts: Beth Ann Masarik (@theworldamongus) and Bilinda Ní Siodacín (@ObsidianMiss)
Time: 4:00 to 5:00 PM EST on Saturdays

#Scifichat
Participants in this chat talk about science fiction literature and the genre in general. The have guest authors join them on occasion.
Host: David Rozansky (@DavidRozansky), publisher of Flying Pen Press
Time: 2:00 to 4:00 PM EST on Fridays

#Scriptchat
Aspiring screenwriters and seasoned pros alike come together to learn from each other in an atmosphere of being in a community rather than being competitors. Each chat, the European GMT one and the American EST one, cover the same topic. Their description advises participants, "Everyone has something to learn, so leave your ego behind."
Hosts: Jeanne V. Bowerman (@jeannevb), Zac Sanford (@zacsanford), @KageyNYC, and @yeah_write.
Times: 8:00 PM GMT and 8:00 PM EST on Sundays
Website: http://scriptchat.blogspot.com

#YAFG
The Young Adult Fantasy Guide discusses YA writing, publishing, book reviews, and social media marketing relevant to the YA fantasy genre.
Host: Stacey O'Neal (YAFantasyGuide)
Time: 9:00 to 10:00 PM EST on Tuesdays
Website: http://www.YAFantasyGuide.com

#YAlitchat
This weekly chat covers young adult literature for both readers and writers.
Hosts: Georgia McBride (@Georgia_McBride) and Lia Keyes (LiaKeyes)
Time: 9:00 to 10:00 PM EST on Wednesdays

These are not the only writing-related chats on Twitter. In addition to them, there are chats on specific topics you might be interested in. A search on Twitter will help you find relevant chats to the topics you write about.

Also note that some of these chats may not be active anymore, but their hashtags are still searchable in the Twitter archives.

For a list of chats on Twitter, check the Google document at the end of the "Schedule of Twitter Chats" at http://swanthinks.wordpress.com/2010/03/02/the-twitter-chat-schedule/

Remember that not all chats are listed on the schedule. For example, there is also #askagent for Ask an Agent chat. However, the person who started that gone a job with a publishing house, so it is no longer a weekly chat but more of a when-someone-thinks-of-it chat.

It is not possible to list all of the hashtags used on Twitter. There are ways to find out if they hashtag you're interested in is in use. The easiest way is to go to Twitter Search and type in "#[tag]" and see what comes up. If it's not in use, use it anyway. It might catch on.

But, how do you connect with other people using the hashtag since that's what Twitter is all about, the connections? There are a few applications you can use.

Twitter Hashtag Applications

There are a few applications you can use along with Twitter that can help you follow what the conversation is around the hashtag you're interested in. Keep in mind that these applications are outside of Twitter and are not a part of the Twitter site. When you use or go to them, you are going off-site even if they use your Twitter username and password to log you in. They will ask your permission before doing this.

Each applications collects the data on the hashtags in a similar fashion, but presents it a little differently depending on layout. The most three popular applications for this purpose are TweetChat, TweetGrid, and TwitterFall.

TweetChat

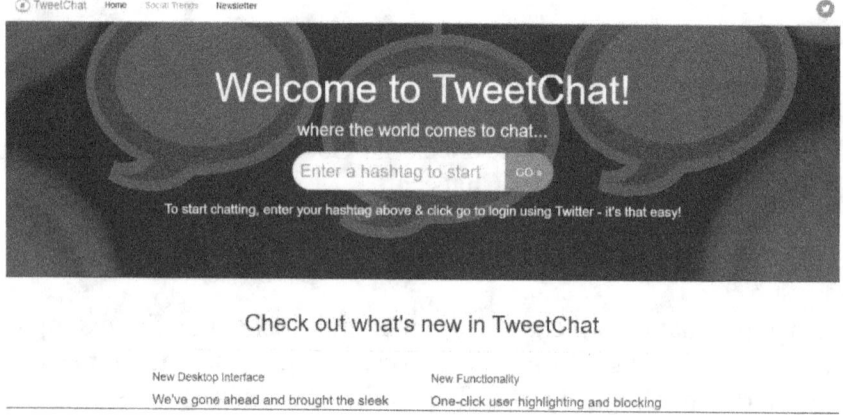

TweetChat is a third party application by oneQube. You can access it at http://www.tweetchat.com.

You must have a Twitter account before you can use this application. If you don't, it will prompt you to sign up with Twitter first. It communicates with Twitter to make sure you are who you say you and that you have an active account. In the center of the login page, you'll also enter the hashtag you want to follow.

For example, even though there's no regular chat, but you want to follow the #amwriting conversation. Enter that hashtag in the field in the middle of the screen and click "Go." When the page loads, you'll have a box for your message with the tag already populated so you don't have to always type it in. Above the box is a place to put URLs you want to shorten.

Under the box, the messages will scroll down with the newest at the top. You can pause the feed if you need to so you can reply to someone in particular.

If you were following a chat, many chats follow a Q&A format with the host presenting questions and the participants offering their viewpoints. To avoid lags while waiting for people to ask questions, many hosts ask for participants to send their questions in advance. If time allows, they will also take questions during the chat.

If you ever want or need a transcript of a particular chat, go back to TweetChat and type in the same hashtag. The previous chats will show up, along with any additional replies or comments people made after the chat was over, providing they used the tag.

There have been improvements in TweetChat since the first edition of this book. They are also working on a TweetChat+Pro. You can sign up for their newsletter for more information on that.

TweetGrid

At the time of this writing, TweetGrid was down. I don't know if this is a temporary thing or if it's down permanently. I present the information I had previously about this third-party app.

You also have to have an active Twitter account to use this application. TweetGrid works in a similar fashion as TweetChat, albeit with a different appearance. This application allows you to have more than one column. You can have a grid anywhere from 1x1 (1 row, 1 column) where all chat messages will appear, to 3x3.

Since Twitter chats have a tendency to be fast-paced, I used a 1x2 so I didn't get lost and I could keep up with what question the comments were replying to. If you didn't enter a specific tag, TweetGrid would stream the entire feed from your home page until you entered the tag you wanted to follow.

The messages there also showed up with the newest at the top.

TwitterFall

One advantage to TwitterFall is that it allows you to follow more than one hashtag at a time. Beware, though, if you're doing this for two simultaneous chats, things can get confusing, particularly if they both move quickly.

Use TwitterFall at http://www.twitterfall.com. Again, be sure you're signed in to Twitter.

At the bottom of the left sidebar is the button to log in using Twitter, then select your tags. In addition, if you have your followers sorted into lists, you can choose which of your lists to watch using TwitterFall as well.

What's This?

A **list** is a way of organizing followers by categories on Twitter. If you follow writers, editors, agents, and public speakers, you can organize them into their respective lists. There is a limit to how many lists you can have. Some people have created new accounts just for the purpose of having more lists available to them.

There are more applications available that follow hashtags and present them in a way that you can use for chat purposes. If nothing else, you can also use the Twitter Search. However, you have to refresh your browser frequently for new messages that show up with that tag.

Chapter 3
Twitter Do's & Don'ts from People Who Have Been There

There are a lot of opinions out there about what writers should and should not do on Twitter. Some argue that basic net etiquette should override the need for any other do's and don'ts. In a way, it does. However, there things specific to writers and writing that really should be covered.

Stacey Graham (@staceyigraham) is a horror writer and literary agent who has made effective use of Twitter. She advises writers, new and otherwise, to participate in chats, such as #agentchat and #querychat. She recommends writers follow publishers, editors, and agents and say hello. She says, "Don't be afraid to ask questions. … Be friendly and chat. She also gives one of the top "don'ts" for Twitter: "DO NOT SELL!"

Heiddi Zalamar (@HeiddiZ), a freelance writer in New York, regularly posts and chats on Twitter. Her advice to writers new to Twitter is, "Share knowledge with other writers and remember that you were a newbie once too."

Dawn Allcot (@dawnallcot), another freelance writer in New York, agrees with the above, but also adds, "Don't whine or worry. Always convey positivity and can-do-it-ness on social media platforms."

Basic Netiquette

No matter where you go in life, there are basic rules of etiquette that apply. The same is true on the Internet, including Twitter.

The most important rule of netiquette is to remember we are all human. It might look like you're interacting with only a screen, but there is another person on the other end. This is true no matter what social media site you use and is not limited only to Twitter. Live broadcasts and other forms of video seem to help remind us of this.

What expectations do you have for yourself and how you behave in real life? What about online? Are they the same? If no, why not? Are your interactions online truly that much different than they are in real life? Just as you wouldn't stalk someone in person, don't stalk them online either. Just because you're in the "cyber" world doesn't make laws irrelevant.

That said, there are some variations site to site. While Twitter is inherently conversational, it is more formal than Facebook, for example. If you're unsure of what standards are accepted in the particular group you want to participate in, lurk and watch what other people do before jumping into the conversation. (I use the term "group" loosely and mean only the people who have similar interests to you on Twitter.)

Be careful what you retweet. Tweets with links to pictures and videos could use too much of someone's bandwidth if a lot of people repost them. Even though there have been advancements in Internet speeds and data usage, limits do still apply and going over them does slow things down.

What's This?

A **retweet** is a repost of what someone else has said on Twitter.

What's This?

> **Bandwidth** is a measure of how a site sends information to your screen from its server.

Always remember your reputation online. This is important for everyone, but especially for writers needing to build their platform. Present a positive impression of who you are and how you want to be seen in everything you do on any social media site. That said, don't try to be someone you aren't. Be yourself.

Share information. You might not think you're an expert in your specific field, but to someone who is just starting in that area, you are. Twitter provides opportunities for you to share the knowledge (read: expertise) you have.

Don't indulge in flame wars. This does not mean you can't express your opinions on whatever is being discussed. When you do, keep yourself in check. Don't let strong emotion accompany your strong opinion, leading someone else to think you're flaming them and reacting in a similar fashion. Repeated posts or tweets like this are what bring about flame wars. On the other hand, occasional flames are acceptable and even expected on the Internet in general.

Some other general points of netiquette include:
- Respect other people's privacy.
- Don't abuse your power/expertise.
- Be forgiving of the mistakes people make.

Face it. We're human. We make mistakes. Forgive them.

Twitter Rules

Kenneth Weene (@ken_weene) a novelist and poet from Phoenix, Arizona, advises writers to follow the 80-10-10 rule. He says, with Twitter and other social media sites, 80% of your posts should be general sharing of information. Then 10% is for promoting your friends and their work. The remaining 10% should be for promoting yourself and your work.

"Of course, it's different if you have a special niche," he says. "Then you can use the 70-10-10-10 rule." The general sharing drops down to 70%. The extra 10% you have now can be used to talk about your specific niche, but not to promote your work in it.

His theory is that if you promote yourself or your friends too much, you will alienate people and lose followers. However, there are many things you can do to lose followers, some more obvious than others.

Chapter 4
Twitter Applications

There are some applications you can use to customize Twitter for your purposes. Some are web-based while others are third-party clients that can be downloaded to your computer. Twitter has made finding applications easy. At the bottom of the Twitter page, you can see a series of links. One says either Widgets or Applications. If you know the web address for the applications site, you can use that as well.

There are mobile applications for your smart phone, web-based applications, and desktop applications. We'll take a look at a few from each category just to give you an idea of what is out there. From that, you should be able to have a good idea of what you're looking for in a Twitter applications and search for one with your preferred features.

Mobile

Twitter for iPhone/Android: These apps stream Twitter in real time, just as the website does. These apps are free to download and use from their respective app stores.

Twitterific http://www.mahalo.com/twitterific: This was Twitter for iPhone before Twitter for iPhone was. It's the first Twitter app to hit the iPhone app store. It's tagline has been "Twitterific puts Twitter in your pocket." With the iPhone, indeed it does. It includes a link-shortening service and tweet translations. You can use it to filter your Twitter stream to specific types of tweets. The app is universal for iPhone and iPad. The initial app is free. However, you can get an in-app purchase of Twitterific Premium, which will remve ads and allow you to manage more than one account.

Ecofon http://www.echofon.com/twitter/iphone: This Twitter app also boasts a clean interface. The initial app is free with the option for an in-app purchase to Ecofon Pro. In addition to real-time streaming, it allows you to mute users and hashtags as well as to preview pictures, videos, etc., in your stream so you can decide if you're interested before viewing the links.

Plume http://levelupstudio/plume: This Android-based Twitter app was formerly known as Touiteur. When Twitter complained about its name, it was changed to Plume. It also allows for previewing media before you commit to seeing it. It lets you manage more than one account and "colorize" your stream. It has free and paid versions.

TweetDeckb http://www.tweetdeck.com/android/: TweetDeck was once a third-party application, but it is now part of Twitter. It works with Twitter, Facebook, FourSquare, and Google Buzz. It allows you to change the vibration, sound, and color alerts you receive for your notifications. (As a side note, there is also TweetDeck for iPhone.) This is a free app.

UberTwitter: This app is available for free in the Blackberry App World. Other than Twitter for Blackberry, this appears to be the most popular Blackberry Twitter app available. It has a clean interface, allows for editing retweets before you send them, and has dialog bubbles on the friends/mentions page.

Blackberry Twitter: This app is also available for free in the Blackberry App World. It promotes the ability to stay connected with the people and information you care about the most. It streams Twitter in real time.

Web-Based

Social Oomph http://www.socialoomph.com: This app offers free and for-fee services. The basic services include scheduling tweets, tracking keywords, shortening links, and deleting all messages from your direct messages folder at once. Additional features include expanding and securing your Twitter profile, saving and reusing drafts, and managing multiple accounts. The site has a simple interface that makes signing up, logging in, and using the site easy to do. Additional features you can get for a fee include automate following new followers back, visiting new followers' profiles, and sending direct messages to new followers. However, I advise against opting in to any automated DM-sending service.

HootSuite http://www.hootsuite.com: This site bills itself as a "Social Media Dashboard." It supports several different social media sites, including Twitter, Facebook, LinkedIn, Ping, WordPress, and Mixi. It has a basic option, which is free, and pro options, for a fee. You can view multiple streams for each account you include. For example, with your Twitter account, you could view the main stream, mentions, direct messages received, direct messages sent, tweets that you sent, and scheduled tweets. It also offers tools so you can view your statistics. However, some of these tools are available only on HootSuite Pro. There are also Firefox and Chrome extensions and addons that can be installed. In addition, there are some choices for downloadable desktop applications as well.

Buffer http://www.bufferapp.com: Buffer is a free web-based app that works with both Twitter and Facebook. If you don't have anything to say, you can click "Suggest an update" and it will auto-populate one for you. They typically say something about using Buffer or sharing a quote. You set the times you want your tweets to go through. However, you can only schedule on tweet per time slot. The purpose of this is so you don't flood your followers with tweets and links if you choose to use it.

Twitterfeed http://www.twitterfeed.com: Import your blogs into your Facebook, LinkedIn, Twitter, and other accounts with Twitterfeed. It's free to register. You need to know the RSS feed address for your blog. Give your feed a name. Enter the feed address and click "continue." You will need to authenticate your account with Twitter so Twitterfeed will have permission to publish the feed to your account. Click "create service." It will take you back to the top of the page so you can add additional accounts if you want to. Otherwise, click "All done." The next page gives you a confirmation of the information you've entered. If it's all correct, go to the Dashboard so you can track your results.

Desktop

TweetDeck http://www.tweetdeck.com: TweetDeck is a rhitd-party platform that streams tweets according to the way you want them. You can have one or more columns. A usual setup has columns for your main Twitter feed, friends, direct messages, and any hashtag searches you have going. The design is a black background with white print. You have to install Adobe Air, free from http://www.adobe.com, for it to run.

Digsby http://www.digsby.com: Digsby is a multi-platform, multi-function application. It allows for feeds and announcements from Twitter, Facebook, LinkedIn, and others. It also collects your email and chat functions, such as ICQ.

Seesmic http://www.seesmic.com: Seesmic is compatible with both PC and Mac operating systems. It has a similar functionality to TweetDeck with multiple columns allowing you to customize how you want to use it.

There are many other third-party mobile, web-based, and desktop Twitter applications. The one that is best for you is the one you find the most user-friendly. Personally, I prefer to use Twitter directly on the website. You might prefer one of the other options discussed here or even another you find yourself.

The idea is to make it as user-friendly for *you* as it can be.

Chapter 5
Benefitting from & Adding Value to Twitter

You have your profile. You know a little bit about hashtags and Twitter applications. You know some do's and don'ts and got a refresher in basic netiquette. Now what? How do you actually use Twitter?

Build Your Network

Why do you need another platform to build your network? After all, you're already on Facebook and LinkedIn, right? (You *are* on LinkedIn, aren't you? We'll talk about a few benefits of that in another chapter.)

Connecting with colleagues, coworkers, friends, and acquaintances on other sites is one thing. Ask yourself this, though: Do they really know what you do?

They might know you're a writer, but do they know *what* you write?

Joining the discussions on Twitter and starting your own discussions will help them figure that out. True, you could simply tell them, but a one-time summary doesn't always stay with people.

We're human. Unless you write it down and give it to us, we honestly might forget it. Then when our company needs an outside person to write advertising copy, for example, we might not remember that you, in fact, write advertorials, brochures, and other such things that we might need.

That doesn't mean that's all you should talk about on Twitter. It does need to be part of your primary discussion, though. In this way, you will become known for it. While networking and gathering people in your network, you will also be building your brand and establishing your niche.

Keep Up with Publishing News and Trends

This does not mean to follow trends so you can write to the trend. We all know that by doing that, you may be too late by the time your article is published.

If you've been around the keyboard for very long, you know things change very quickly in the publishing world. Following other writers editors, publishers, and literary agents on Twitter helps you say up-to-date with the latest—or upcoming—changes. Industry watch-dogs, such as Writer Beware and Preditors & Editors, also have Twitter accounts.

Exactly who you want to follow depends on your writing focus. If you write children's books, you would follow different people than I do with writing nonfiction and romance. Some agents, editors, and other industry professionals are listed in the appendices in the back.

Here is a true story to illustrate the benefit you can get from following industry professionals. A few years ago, I decided to start a separate Twitter account for my romance-writing pen name. I put my pen name, real name, and a short bio up first. Then I went to work on my profile design. By the time I got that finished, I had a message from a small press that was interested in my work and requesting me to send an email with more details. I did. He requested the full manuscript.

It was ultimately rejected, but I still participate in many discussions he has on Twitter and count him a valuable resource.

Get Inspired

While it's true that ideas are everywhere, it's also true that sometimes, for any variety of reasons, we don't see them as quickly as we normally do.

This is another time when using Twitter search can be helpful. Do a search on the topic you want to write about or a new one you're interested in pursuing. You can use the hashtag or not. For search purposes, it doesn't really matter.

Click all the links that come up until you find something that really piqwues your interest. That means you don't get too involved in the ones that seem only "kinda" neat. (I've done this before and came across and article titled "50 Kloutless Ways to Get Value from Twitter" by Lisa Barone. Part of this chapter was inspired by that article.

Once you have an idea that sparks your interest to the point that it feels like an electric shock from a wall outlet, run with it. What about it grabbed you by the throat and won't let go? Look at it from every possible angle and work it.

No, using an article or blog post as inspiration is not plagiarism. You're not copying it word-for-word. You're using the idea behind it to fuel your own writing. Trust me, you're not the only writer who will ever do that. More often than not, you'll write about a different angle. Or you'll write a novel based on the idea from a short blog post. I've heard other writers compare Twitter to a writers' conference you can go to at your convenience.

Talk to Your Readers

Yes, you have readers. Even if you're not yet published in the area you prefer, you still have potential readers. If you have a blog, you definitely have readers. Get them involved in your discussions. This serves two immediate purposes: It gets your name out there and lets them know what you're about. They go to your website and/or blog. You want them to go there. While you will give them updates on Twitter, your blog and website are the places they will find more details on the news you use to tease them and get them to click your links.

Plus, getting your readers involved in your discussions also works to your advantage if you are a freelance writer looking for work. Of course, you don't hit them over the head with that fact, but you'll be on their radar, so they will be more likely to click through and check out your services if they ever find they have need for your specialty.

Answer Questions

People tend to tweet questions about problems they are having. If you see a question from someone in your Twitter stream and you know how you can help them either reply or send them a direct message. Replying publicly gets your name and expertise in the Twitter stream in general, which could be more advantageous for you.

On the flip side, if you have a problem, post it. You might be surprised at all of the suggestions you get. However, be prepared for spam links and general irrelevant information. People generally mean well, but they're not always as well-versed in your particular problem as they think they might be.

Answering questions helps increase your visibility and credibility. Asking questions helps you appear human and avoid looking like a know-it-all. As a bit of an aside, asking questions can also help you find new sources for articles.

Tell Your Stories

Remember Twitter is not all about you. With that said, sometimes it is appropriate to share your own experiences over the course of a chat or other discussion.

Not only that, but sometimes you can present your stories in a blog post and offer a teaser and a link on Twitter. It's also a good outlet for recycling stories and articles that you didn't use before.

But wait!

Don't just put everything up on a blog and give a link. For one, if you post nothing but links and don't add anything else to any of the conversations, you could well be ignored and possibly lose followers.

Remember what I said about editors being on Twitter? So are magazines. Some of them provide a link to their guidelines. Check and see if they would be appropriate for the article or post you have gathering cyber dust on your hard drive.

If they're not appropriate, or if you decide to put it on your blog anyway, go for it. I only suggest that you be careful about how often you post links. There is no real rule about that and it depends on how often you post. If you only post once a day, I would suggest only posting one link a week.

Listen.

There is a saying for face-to-face interaction that goes something like this: "God gave you two ears and one mouth, so you should listen twice as much as you talk."

The flip side to that seems to be the standard mode of operation in online interactions: "God gave you two eyes and ten fingers, so you can post five times as much as you read." Right?

Wrong!

If you're posting more than you're reading, you're not paying attention to what's going on. You're not participating in any discussions. You're too busy posting links, sending pictures (notice I didn't say "sharing"), and generally all but screaming "LOOK AT ME!"

That will get you ignored. Over time, it will get you unfollowed. And it certainly will not get you any potential assignments or invitations to submit with instructions on how to bypass the gatekeepers.

Share Your Expertise

If you're anything like I used to be, you might be thinking, "I'm not an expert at anything."

I disagree.

If, for example, you enjoy fly fishing, but you only discovered it a year ago, you're still an expert to someone who started yesterday.

Sharing your expertise includes answering questions people post. Don't look at it as giving away free stuff but as gaining new readers for your books and articles. Although, with the emphasis now on giving freebies to your readers and subscribers, looking at it as a freebie might not necessarily be a bad thing.

Go Off-Topic

As another saying goes, "All work and no play make Jack a dull boy." Keep that in mind regarding Twitter as well.

Go off-topic from time to time. Post pictures. Tell jokes. Just remember your platform at all times and keep it in line with the image you want to project.

When you show you're willing to talk about other things than your niche, you appear more approachable.

Overwhelmed?

Don't be. Above all, Twitter is a pretty straight-forward platform despite frequent changes. There's nothing that says you have to read this book cover-to-cover and memorize it all before you get started.

In fact, don't do that.

The best way to learn Twitter and get comfortable with is is to use it, not just read about it.

Chapter 6
Avoiding the Time-Sink

One common complaint I hear about Twitter and other social media sites is they take too much time. It can be. I won't argue with that. I've spent too much time chasing links on more than one occasion.

There is nothing that says you can't do your social media tasks in about 20 minutes a day. Yes, 20 minutes. It's not easy at first but it does pay off. (Also note that this does not include any chats you might decide to participate in on Twitter.) Here is a three-step plan I've been following. Try it and see if it works for you.

Setting Your Twitter Schedule

1. Make a to-do list.
Do this first thing in the morning either before you turn your computer on or while waiting for it to boot up. (Alternatively, make your list the night before.) Ideally, this should take no more than two to five minutes. You don't want to overwhelm yourself with things you "need" to do.

What are three to five things you want to do in building your social media presence today? (Or tomorrow?) List only one thing per line.

_____
_____
_____

What are some social media tasks you can include on your to-do list? Writing a blog post, researching new social media tools (whether for Twitter, Facebook, LinkedIn, etc.), and attending a webinar are just a few things you might include.

2. Set hourly alarms to check how you're doing.

This assumes that you took a few minutes to do the things on your list. You can't see how many people clicked through to read your blog post if you didn't write and post it.

Use the calendar on your computer or the alarms on your phone to set hourly alerts. When it goes off, check how you're doing. Do you need to redirect or refocus?

Throughout the day, this will take a minute at a time. By the end of the day, you will have spent about ten minutes on refreshing and redirecting.

3. Review how you did.

In the evening, as you're getting ready to put an end to the day, review how you did. These are some specific things you can address:

- How did your day go?
- What did you learn?
- Who did you interact with?
- Did you get any new followers? If so, did you send them a quick @ reply to thank them for following you?
- Did someone retweet you, repost your link, or otherwise mention you? If so, did you send them a quick @ reply to thank them?

These questions will help you figure out what needs to go on your to-do list for the next day. This day-end review should take place after you turn your computer off. That way, you won't be tempted to get back online "real quick" and do the things you might not have done. Trust me; they can wait until morning.

Additional Tips

Say "no."
We take on too much in our daily lives. It's no different online. Unless you are positive you can juggle multiple accounts without falling back into the time sink, don't jump on every social media platform out there. If you're on Facebook and Twitter, that's good enough to start. (Later on, I would recommend adding LinkedIn, but that's now for now.) You have two venues in which you can interact with friends, colleagues, and industry professionals. Call it good.

Use a calendar.
As a writer, you have specific things going on at different points throughout the year. Use a calendar to help you keep track of when you need to start getting the word out about the. What conferences are you to attending or speaking at? Do you think anyone in your Twitter stream would want to know about that? Figure out how much advanced notice you want to give and start tweeting information and additional details as they become available (meaning whenever you decide they can be given without jumping the gun too much).

Manage time before distractions set in.
Writing is basically a solitary profession. Yes, we have critique groups we go to and conferences we can attend, but when it gets right down to it, there isn't anyone else sitting at the keyboard with us. It's easy to fall into a trap of going online for a few minutes before you get started and later find an hour (or more) has passed. Figuring out how to manage your online time will help avoid those distractions. I would never presume to say you won't fall prey to them, but you'll realize it when you do. Managing your time online has the added benefit that it will also help to organize the rest of your day and assist in time management in other areas as well.

If you were feeling a little overwhelmed, does this help some? It will take practice to get the system working for you so that it truly only takes 20 minutes a day. It's also possible that you might find this system doesn't work for you. That's fine. If nothing else, it gave you a starting point to figure out what you want to do on your social media platforms and how to go about organizing them to benefit you and your followers.

Let me just say this is definitely easier said than done. Just when I think I have the system mastered, something (or someone) throws a monkey wrench into the works. (In the interest of full disclosure, *I* am usually that someone.)

Chapter 7
Your First Tweets

This is the chapter *you* will write. Yes, I want you to take a few minutes and really think this through.

List five topic areas you can talk about on Twitter.
1. _____
2. _____
3. _____
4. _____
5. _____

Now take a minute and write an introductory tweet about yourself. Remember, you have only 280 characters, including spaces and punctuation.

_____
_____
_____
_____

Don't worry if it isn't perfect. It doesn't have to be. In fact, it's probably better if it isn't. Go ahead and post it if you're relatively happy with it.

Get "Twitter"pated

Take your five topics you listed above. Write out a tweet or two for them.

Topic 1:

_____
_____
_____
_____

Good. Keep going.

Topic 2:

_____
_____
_____
_____

Topic 3:

_____
_____
_____
_____

Topic 4:

_____
_____
_____
_____

Topic 5:

_____
_____
_____
_____

Congratulations! You have just written this chapter of the book.

And, more importantly, you have at least six tweets, maybe up to 11 (counting your introductory one) ready to post.

The rest is up to you. Keep posting, finding interesting people in our areas of interest to follow, and interacting. It's the interacting that's key. Without it, you're talking to air.

Appendix A

Glossary

bandwidth: a measure of how a site sends information to your screen from its server

direct message: Twitter's private in-site message service that follows the same character limit

hashtag #: a tag that enables Twitter to be searched and chats to be followed

list: a way of organizing followers by categories on Twitter

MT: a modified tweet, used when the original tweet is too long and changes had to be made; use very sparingly

retweet: a repost of what someone else has said on Twitter

RT: abbreviation for retweet

tweet: a post on Twitter limited to 280 characters, including spaces and punctuation

Twitter feed or **stream:** the page of tweets from everyone you follow on Twitter that you see when you click on the home page after you log in

Twitter Search: Twitter's own search engine that looks for keywords among any and all public tweets
http://search.twitter.com

Appendix B

People Mentioned

32 Poems	@32poems
Abbott, Charlotte	@charabbott
Adamson, Bonnie	@BonnieAdamson
Allcot, Dawn	@dawnallcot
Apple, Linda	@write_2_inspire
Bowerman, Jeanne V.	@jeannevb
Christianson, Claudia	@ClaudiaC
Collier, Mack	@mackcollier
Evans, Sarah	@PRSarahEvans, @journchat
Graham, Stacey	@staceyigraham
Keyes, Lia	@LiaKeyes
Masarik, Beth Ann	@theworldamongus
McBride, Georgia	@Georgia_McBride
Meyer, Kat	@kaymeyer
Muniz, Marilyn	@marilynmuniz
Ní Siodacín, Bilinda	@ObsidianMiss
O'Neal, Stacey	@YAFantasyGuide
Pincus, Greg	@gregpincus
Rozansky, David	@DavidRozansky
Sanford, Zac	@zacsanford
Weene, Kenneth	@ken_weene
Wright, Keri	@fantasychat
Zalamar, Heiddi	@HeiddiZ

Appendix C

Related Books

All a Twitter: A Personal and Professional Guide to Social Networking with Twitter
Tee Morris
Que
2009
ISBN: 978-0-789-74228-5

Getting Started with Twitter
Laura Fitton, Michael Gruen, and Leslie Poston
Wiley Publishing Inc.
2009
ISBN: 978-0-470-55176-9

Social Media Marketing for Dummies
Shiv Singh
Wiley Publishing, Inc.
2010
ISBN: 978-0-470-58535-0

Socialnomics: How Social Media Transforms the Way We Live and Do Business
Erik Qualman
Wiley Publishing, Inc.
2009
ISBN: 978-0-470-52180-9

The Twitter Book
Tim O'Reilly and Sarah Milstein
O'Reilly Media
2009
ISBN: 978-0-596-80281-3

Twitter for Dummies
Laura Fitton, Michael Gruen, and Leslie Poston
Wiley Publishing, Inc.
2009
ISBN: 978-0-470-47991-9

Twitter Marketing an Hour a Day
Hollis Thomases
Sybex
2010
ISBN: 978-0-478-56226-0

Twitter Marketing for Dummies
Kyle Lacey
For Dummies
2009
ISBN: 978-0-470-56172-0

Twitter Power 2.0: How to Dominate Your Market One Tweet at a Time
Joel Comm
Wiley Publishing, Inc.
2010
ISBN: 978-0-470-56336-6

Twitter Tips, Tricks, and Tweets
Paul McFedries
Wiley Publishing, Inc.
2010 (2nd edition)
ISBN: 978-0-470-62466-1

Appendix D

Book Publishers on Twitter

While this list is extensive, it is not exhaustive. There are publishers on Twitter that are not on this list. Do your homework with any publisher you are interested in. Check the industry watchdogs, including Writer Beware and Preditors & Editors for any complaints or warnings about a publisher before you approach them.

Alfred A. Knopf	@AAKnopf
Abbeville Press	@Abbeville
Abingdon Press	@AbingdonPress
Affirm Press	@affirmpress
Algonquin Books	@AlgonquinBooks
The Alternate Press	@AlternatePress
Alyson Books	@alysonbooks
Ambassador International	@AmbassadorIntl
Amber Quill Press	@AmberQuillPress
American Management Association	@AMACOMBooks
American Book Publishing	@AmericanBook
A Midsummer Night's Press	@AMidsummerNight
AMMO Books	@ammobooks
Andrews McMeel Publishing	@AndrewsMcMeel
Annick Press	@AnnickPress
Annova Books	@AnnovaBooks
Apostrophe Books	@ApostropherBooks
Aquarius Press	@AquariusPress

Arcade Publications	@arcadegazette
Arsenal Pulp	@ArsenalPulp
Atria Books	@AtriaBooks
Auldhouse Publishing	@auldhouse
Aurum Press	@aurumpress
Beacon Press	@BeaconPressBks
BenBella Books	@benbellabooks
Broadman Holman Publishing Group	@BHpub
Bilingual Readers	@bilingualrdrs
Black Inc.	@blackincbooks
Bloomsbury Publishing	@BloomsburyBooks
British Library Publishing	@BLPublishing
Brascoe Publishing	@brascoebooks
Brick Books	@brickbooks
Camber Press	@CamberPress
Candlewick Press	@candlewick
Canongate	@canongatebooks
Capstone Publishing	@thisiscapstone
Center Street	@centerstreet
Champagne Books	@champagnebooks
Charlesbridge	@charlesbridge
Chelsea Green Publishing	@chelseagreen
Lake Claremont Press	@ChicagoPress
Chicago Review Press	@ChiReviewPress
Chicken Soup for the Soul series (Simon & Schuster)	@chickensoupsoul
Chronicle Books	@ChronicleBooks
Cisco Press	@ciscopress
Clavis Books	@clavisbooks
Coach House Books	@coachhousebooks
Coffee House Press	@Coffee_House_
Columbia University Press	@ColumbiaUP
Conari Press	@ConariPress
Crown Publishing	@crownpublishing
Damnation Books	@DamnationBooks
Dark Horse Comics	@DarkHorseComics
Destin World Publishing	@destinworld
Discovery House	@discoveryhouse
DKBooks	@DKBooks

Doubleday Publishing	@doubledaypub
Dragon Moon Press	@dragonmoonpress
Duke University Press	@DUKEpress
The Dundurn Group	@dundurnpress
Dutton Books	@DuttonBooks
Dzanc Books	@DzancBooks
Ebury Publishing	@eburypublishing
Ecco Books	@EccoBooks
Echelon Press	@echelonpress
ECW Press	@ecwpress
Egmont UK	@Egmontbooks
Egmont USA	@EgmontUSA
ENC Press	@ENCPress
EosBooks	@EosBooks
Eternal Press	@EternalPress
Exisle Publishing	@exislebooks
Faber & Faber	@FaberBooks
FaithWords	@faithwords
Fantagraphics Books	@fantagraphics
Farcountry Press	@farcountrypress
The Feminist Press	@FeministPress
Free Press	@freepressbooks
Friends of ED	@friendsofED
Fodor's Travel	@fodorstravel
Frontenac House	@poetlariatt
Ford Street Publishing	@fordstreet
For Dummies	@ForDummies
Forever	@foreverromance
Financial Times Prentice Hall	@FTPH
Graphic Arts Center Publishing Company	@GACPC_books
Gray Dog Press	@gdpeditor
Grand Central Publishing	@GrandCentralPub
Graywolf Press	@GraywolfPress
Griffyn Ink Publishing	@GriffynInk
Groundwood Books	@GroundwoodBooks
Grove Atlantic, Inc.	@groveatlantic
Hades Publications, Inc.	@HadesPub
Harlequin Books Digital Team	@HarlequinBooks
Hardie Grant Books	@hardiegrantbook

HarperAcademic	@HarperAcademic
HarperBooks Australia	@HarperBooksAus
HarperCollins Children's Books	@harperchildrens
HarperCollins Canada	@HarperCollinsCa
HarperOne	@harperone
HarperStudio	@harperstudio
HarperCollins Teen Division	@harperteen
Haymarket Books	@haymarketbooks
Head First Labs, O'Reilly Media	@headfirstlabs
Hersilia Press	@hersilia_press
Holyridge Press	@HolyridgePress
House of Anansi	@HouseofAnansi
Iambikaudiobooks	@iambikaudio
Icon Books	@iconbooks
Inner Traditions	@InnerTraditions
Island Press	@IslandPress
Indiana University Press	@iupress
InterVarsity Press	@IVPress
JosseyBass Parenting	@JBParenting
JosseyBass Business	@JosseyBassBiz
Kallisti Publishing	@KallistiPublish
Kaplan Publishing	@ReadKaplan
Kensington Books	@Kensingtonbooks
Kumarian Press	@kumarianpress
Last Gasp Books	@lastgaspbooks
Lee and Low Books	@LEEandLOW
Little Brown and Co.	@littlebrown
Macmillan Kids	@MacKidsBooks
Maupin House	@MaupinHouse
McArthur and Company	@McArthurCo
The McGrawHill Companies	@mcgrawhillcos
Medallion Press	@MedallionPress
Melville House	@melvillehouse
Mercury Retrograde Press	@mercuryrx
McGrawHill Professional	@mhbusiness
Microsoft Press	@MicrosoftPress
Milkweed Editions	@Milkweed_Books
Minotaur Books	@MinotaurBooks
Pogue Press	@missingmanuals
MIT Press	@mitpress

The Monacelli Press	@MonacelliPress
Morrigan Books	@morriganbooks
Mulholland Books	@mulhollandbooks
Muumuu House	@muumuuhouse
Mysterious Press	@eMysteries
Nation Books	@nationbooks
Thomas Nelson Inc.	@ThomasNelson
Newmarket Press	@NewmarketPress
New World Library	@newworldlibrary
North Atlantic Books	@NAtlanticBooks
Northwestern University Press	@NorthwesternUP
W.W. Norton	@NortonAnthology
	@NortonCriticals
	@norton_fiction
NYRB Classics	@nyrbclassics
New York University Press	@NYUpress
Ocean Publishing	@OceanPub
Octopus Publishing Group	@Octopus_Books
Open Letter (University of Rochester)	@open_letter
Michael O'Mara Books	@OmaraBooks
Orbit Books	@orbitbooks
O'Reilly Media	@oreillymedia
Other Press	@otherpress
Oxford University Press	@oupblogusa
Our Little Books	@ourlittlebooks
Overlook Press	@overlookpress
Packt Publishing	@packtpub
Pan Macmillan Australia	@panmacmillanaus
Paper Bag Press	@paperbagpress
Peachpit Press	@peachpit
Peach Tree Publishing	@peachtreepub
Pear Press	@pearpress
Pearson	@pearson
PenguinBooks	@PenguinBooks
Penguin Books Australia	@penguinbooksaus
Penguin Canada	@PenguinCanada
Penguin Classics	@PenguinClassics
PenguinTeen	@PenguinTeen
Penguin Group (USA)	@penguinusa

Phaze Books	@phazeromance
Picador Australia	@picadoraus
Picador	@picadorbooks
Picador Paperbacks	@picadorusa
Platypus Media	@PlatypusMedia
Pluto Press	@plutopress
Pocket Books	@Pocket_Books
Polity	@politybooks
The Porcupine's Quill	@pocupinesquill
powerHouse Books	@powerHouseBooks
Prestel	@Prestel_UK
Pyr Books	@pyr_books
Quake	@quakeme
Random House	@randomhouse
Random House of Canada, Digital Team	@RandomHouseCA
Random House Australia	@randomreaders
Recliner Books	@ReclinerBooks
Red Rock Press	@redrockpress
Riverhead Books	@riverheadbooks
Rocky Mountain Books	@rmbooks1
Roaring Forties Press	@Roaring40sPress
Saqi & Telegram	@saqibooks
Sarabande Books	@sarabandebooks
Scholastic Canada	@ScholasticCda
Science, Naturally!	@SciNaturally
Scribe Publications	@scribepub
Self-Counsel Press	@SelfCounsel
Sentient Publications	@Sentient_Pub
Simon & Schuster Canada	@SimonSchusterCA
Simon & Schuster	@simonschuster
Simon & Schuster Australia	@simonschusterau
Sleepers	@sleepersublish
Snowbooks	@snowbooks
Spinifex Press	@spinifexpress
Strang Book Group	@StrangBookGroup
Sydney University Press	@SydneyUniPress
Taylor and Francis	@tandfbooks
Tarcher/Penguin	@TarcherBooks
Text Publishing	@text_publishing

Thunder Bay Press	@ThunderBayBooks
Tindal Street Press	@tindalstreet
Tin House Books	@TinHouseBooks
Tor Books	@torbooks
Tor Teen	@torteen
Trapdoor Books	@TrapdoorBooks
TSTC Publishing	@tstcpublishing
Tundra Books	@TundraBooks
Tyndale House Publishers	@TyndaleHouse
Unbridled Books	@unbridledbooks
Union Square Press	@UnionSqPress
University of California Press	@UCPress
University of Chicago Press	@UChicagoPress
University of Michigan Press	@UofMPress
University of Minnesota Press	@UMinnPress
University of North Carolina Press	@uncpressblog
University of Toronto Press	@utpress
Veloce Publishing	@Velocebooks
VeloPress	@velopress
Viking Books	@VikingBooks
Vintage/Anchor	@VintageAnchor
Vintage Books	@vintagebooks
Wallflower Press	@wallflowerpress
Walnut Springs Press	@walnutspringspr
Weiser Books	@WeiserBooks
Whitecap Books	@whitecapbooks
Wiley Business Books	@wileybiz
Wiley (lifestyle titles)	@lifestylePR
Wiley Canada	@WileyCanada
Wiley Tech	@WileyTech
WordFarm	@wordfarmbooks
Workman Publishing	@WorkmanPub
Wrox	@Wrox
Yale Press	@yalepress
ZestBooks	@ZestBooks
Zondervan Academic	@ZonderAcademic
Zondervan Publishers	@Zondervan

About the Author

Jen Nipps writes from her home in south-central Oklahoma. She has been on Twitter since July 2008. She is an award-winning poet and author with a wide variety of interests that influence her writing. She gives presentations on various topics related to writing, creativity, social media, and blogging.

Other Books By Jen Nipps

Devoted to Creating: Igniting the Creative Spark in Everyone
Currently out of print

Windsong & Other Poems

80 Creativity Tips

Create Your Own DIY Planner

Project Planner for Creatives

8 Patterns to Crochet

Journal Your Way to Creativity

Written as Kat O'Reilly

Navajo Rose

Kiernan's Curse

Connect with Jen Online

Email: jennippsonline@gmail.com

Website/Blog: www.jennippsonline.com

Facebook: www.facebook.com/byjennipps

Twitter: www.twitter.com/JenNipps

LinkedIn: www.linkedin.com/in/jennipps

Sign up for Jen's email list to learn about upcoming books, events, and social media tips.

www.ingramcontent.com/pod-product-compliance
Lightning Source LLC
Chambersburg PA
CBHW071111240526
45469CB00006BD/2433